MOM, WHAT IS THE OPPOSITE OF GUACAMOLE?

A BOOK OF HILARIOUS AND THOUGHTFUL KIDS' QUOTES

KELLY STONE

Copyright © 2021 Kelly Stone.

All rights reserved. No part of this book may be used or reproduced by any means, graphic, electronic, or mechanical, including photocopying, recording, taping or by any information storage retrieval system without the written permission of the author except in the case of brief quotations embodied in critical articles and reviews.

Archway Publishing books may be ordered through booksellers or by contacting:

Archway Publishing
1663 Liberty Drive
Bloomington, IN 47403
www.archwaypublishing.com
844-669-3957

Because of the dynamic nature of the Internet, any web addresses or links contained in this book may have changed since publication and may no longer be valid. The views expressed in this work are solely those of the author and do not necessarily reflect the views of the publisher, and the publisher hereby disclaims any responsibility for them.

ISBN: 978-1-4808-7320-9 (sc)
ISBN: 978-1-4808-7321-6 (hc)
ISBN: 978-1-4808-7319-3 (e)

Library of Congress Control Number: 2018914728

Print information available on the last page.

Archway Publishing rev. date: 04/23/2021

Contents

Preface ix
Introduction xiii

Givers of Advice 1
Old Souls 7
Texans 19
Dude Bros 29
Engineers 35
Relationship Experts 41
Scientists 53
Existential Philosophers 61
Forward Thinkers 75
Sweet, Sweet Angels 85
Assholes 97
Grossers 113
In Mom's Shoes 119

Acknowledgements 125
About the Author 127
About the Boys 129

For **Mayne** and **Den**ly.

You dudes have exponentially expanded my questioning of the universe, and I am humbly grateful.

Preface

Friends,

I'm tickled to meet you, and I'm especially honored that you purchased this book. It's my first. I sure as heck hope it won't be my last. I've wanted to write a book for as long as I can remember. I got awards for my writing in junior high and high school, and some day, I will try to prove to y'all why I may have been considered a decent writer. This book is not for that. Thanks for supporting me early in my authorship journey, but the words and language in this book did not come from my skull though I do take credit for having the wherewithal to write all this stuff down.

I also take credit for the space I've created through my (flawed) parenting that my kids have been comfortable asking questions about anything and everything, and I guess it's also probably my fault that they have absolutely no filter for their thoughts. They just tell it like they see it. So, over the years, I jotted down the stuff my kids prattled off here and there. I'd scribble in a notebook or fire off a tweet or FB post immediately after their kiddo brains crafted something that made me laugh or cringe.

Honestly, I never wanted or intended to be a mom, and every single day of being one is an adjustment. It's exhausting because I'm not maternal or nurturing or prepared with all the things. Also, it's exhausting. I merely try my hardest to keep them healthy, happy, and alive, and so far...so good?

One Monday, I captured all of the following quotes from just one of the children:

"Mom, why is it so bad to be called a girl?"

"How am I supposed to talk to my kids in the future about Santa without actual video proof that he's real?"

"Why does everybody wonder what I'm thinking about?"

"Mom, what makes semen come out?"

"Mom, who discovered Santa?"

"Mom, can't you just do it all yourself?"

"Mom, what is the opposite of guacamole?"

I was tired. It was a long Monday.

Eventually, folks were stopping me on the street (sidewalk) to tell me how funny they thought these posts were. This encouraged me to quote them more often, adding up to roughly 8 years of collecting these gems!

I had a lot of fun putting this together, and I hope you have fun reading and sharing it with others. Seriously. I'm still a single mom, and this is basically a lot of eggs in that college savings basket for these guys. So, thank you for buying up several copies of this book as gifts for every baby shower ever. (OMG! THANK YOU!) You are a true feminist and ally, and I (we) genuinely appreciate your support.

Cheers!

K. Stone

Introduction

This book is broken up into the types of roles or personae my boys were embodying when they said each of these things. They can say the sweetest stuff you could possibly imagine, and they will also call me fat and pick on my body. They vacillate between idealists and realists, little buddhists and big conspiracists, and they pull no punches with their observations or thoughts.

These quotes will make you laugh and shake your head, most likely at the same time. Enjoy.

Givers of Advice

> Mom, this is all just normal life. It's not a party. You don't need to be so excited.

> Hey Mom, turn your headlights on.

> Mom, thank you so much for letting us stay up so late[1]! Is it after midnight[2] yet?

---

[1] It was Daylight Savings.
[2] It was 8:30 pm.

> Mom, what time do you want to go skinny-dipping in the full moon for your birthday?

> Mom, I think that my fear of sharks started when you put my placenta in the river. I'm pretty sure a shark ate it.

> Mom, I'm pretty sure I'm going to need to talk to a therapist in the future, and I'm gonna need like 5 hours cuz I have a lot to say.

{ "Mom, do you think I'm evolving into a comedian?" }

{ "Mom, I need at least 30 hugs per day." }

Old Souls

> Me: "Do you know what you wanna be when you grow up?"
> Kid: "Yeah! A grown up!"

> Mom, I don't wanna go to the movies and see The Muppets! I want to stay home and watch Devil Wears Prada!

"Mom, I should start flying by myself more often. I really like seeing new places and having new experiences."

"Mom, I'm putting together my own dinner. Alright, Missy?!"

"Mom, are these military bunk beds actually from the military?" "Yep." "Then they've definitely been puked on."

"No, Mom, in my Bible, it says that people are the bosses of themselves and that we don't have to worry about other people. That's what it says."

> Mom, can we please use the self check-out station because that lady looks mean. I mean, I can tell from her hair that she's had a very stressful day.

> Mom, I just woke up thinking about who was elected president.

" "Mom, can you read this to me?"
"Hmmm...can you try to read it to me?"
(loudly) "A t-timed---tammd--tamed mind. A tamed mind brings happiness."
(Younger son loudly from other room) "No, bro, you read that wrong! A tamed mind *drains* happiness. Not brings! DRAINS!"

> Mom, I promise, I never lie. But *sometimes* I lie.

> Mom, I don't know why, but I just feel like I'm a grown-up already. I mean, I already know how to do everything by myself without help. I can tie my shoes. I can read. I can do math. I can do everything! I just need help with my homework.

> Mom, I don't know why you're giving me a reward for finishing 2nd grade. I didn't do anything. I just copied what the teacher wanted, and I've forgotten it all already. I don't deserve anything.

"

Mom, you're just throwing tacos at me.

"

"

Mom, am I too strong for my age?

"

> Mom, I wish third grade wasn't like a *thing*, you know? I mean, why can't I just like get a house and stuff already?

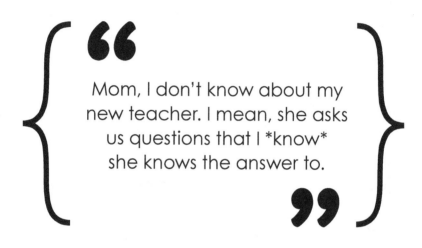

"Mom, I don't know about my new teacher. I mean, she asks us questions that I *know* she knows the answer to."

"Mom, why do they have cake at funerals?"

> Mom, it's for the best that I didn't get a tattoo when I was three because I prolly would've gotten a unicorn or a dinosaur or a rainbow, and I would've been like 'why did I get that dinosaur on a rainbow', you know? Man, I love these earrings.

> Mom, please turn off NPR. I just woke up, and I can't handle hearing radio people whine about the government right now.

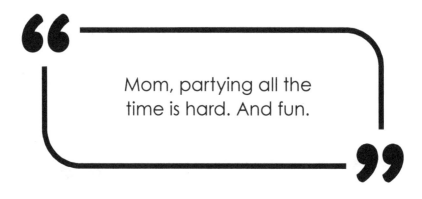

"Mom, partying all the time is hard. And fun."

"Mom, can someone get famous for making lots of mixtapes?"

Texans

{ "Mom, hurry, I want to get outside to play in the Denver snow before it melts." }

{ "Hi River, I love you so much!"
"River, I love you with all my heart and soul."
"And River, my mom will always be on your side." }

> Mom, can we have a dune buggy so we can fly ourselves to the unicycle football games?

> Magenta is Spanish for purple, right Mom?

"Mom, parade floats are just very, very big wagons."

> Mom, my lips are red, like fiery red, like bald eagle American red.

> See Mom, it's a frozen basketball field cuz you can see the lines.

Mom, thanks for getting us this trampoline. It was exactly what was missing from our bedroom.

Mom, would you say that me running Rio Vista in a K2 is newsworthy? Because I think everybody should know.

> Mom, I think I'm actually Mexican. I mean, I really love Mexican food a lot, so I probably have ancestors from Mexico.

{
Mom, wasn't I so brave at the dentist? I just kept thinking about unicorns and rainbows in their butts. Oh, and snipe rifles.
 }

{
Mom, I discovered what my talents are this weekend. Yeah, it's shooting. I'm really good at shooting guns.
 }

> Mom, I know I look all sweet and nice, but I'm really a weight-lifting, bag-punching kinda kid.

> Mom, I actually don't need knife skills for survival cuz haven't you heard of...um, hello? HEB?!

Dude Bros

> Mom, Mom, Mom! I made lots of poopies! Come look! Are you proud of me?

> Here, Mom, let me help you with that heavy bag. I got this cuz I didn't even play at recess. I just worked out instead.

"Mom, today at school we had to come up with things to describe ourselves using the letters in our names. I really wanted to say that I'm funny, but there's no F in my name. So, instead, I used the Y, and I wrote 'Yo momma funny'."
"What did you put down for the letter D?"

"D: Dolls creep me out."

Mom, did you know I can flex my
buttocks much harder than my arms?

"Mom, look at this picture my brother just took."
"Why would you take a picture of your penis?"
"To be hilarious!"

Engineers

> Mom, you know what I think would make Wendy's menu better? If they sold Church's Chicken.

> Hey, Mom, look! I just made this acid bomb.

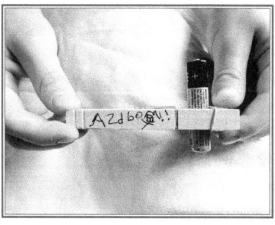

Mom, this breakfast burrito is delicious! Have they invented something called a 'lunch burrito'?

Mom, come look! The ceiling exploded while we were sleeping!

> Mom, I really care about this table, and I don't want it to get messed up. That's why I put my drink on this towel.

> "Mom, why would Donald Trump get rid of PBS Kids to build a wall against Mexico? Mexico is great. They have nice beaches. And tacos. Why isn't he trying to build like a radio-wall against Russia?"

> "Mom, we're pretending we are famous marble track builders, and do you know all those twists and turns in Las Vegas? That's our inspiration."

> *holding dustbuster* Mom, we just figured out how to make the best ponytail ever!

Relationship Experts

> Mom, moms don't have balls, right?

> Mom, I like this bus driver cuz he lets us sit wherever we want, and I sat next to a really pretty girl.

> Mom, your belly looks pregnant. (Sigh) I really wish we had a sister.

> Mom, I don't know Katie from my class very well. Do you think that if I bring her jewelry, she will love me?

> "Mom, don't freak out, but I have a crush on a 5th grader."
> "Oh, what's their name?"
> "I dunno."
> "What do you like about this 5th grader?"
> "The way she looks."
> "Oh? What does she look like?"
> "A tall hyena."

> Mom, what are those clubs for girls called? Aren't they just called 'Vaginas'?

> Mom, did you know that Donald Trump hates women? I don't hate women. Someday when I grow up, maybe I'll be a woman. Or maybe I'm a girl now, and I'll grow up to be a man. I mean, we all have bladders.

> Mom, I don't care if girls take off their shirts. It's really just like me with no shirt. I mean, nipples are just hairy dots.

> Mom, why are you drawing a picture to tell us you have a different pee hole? Can't you just show us?

> Mom, why do I have girl shoulders?

> Mom, what does 'married'
> even mean really?

> Mom, I kinda don't think you'll want
> to answer this question. It's a little
> crazy actually, so I don't even think
> I should ask...but, okay, here it is:
> Who invented childbirth?

> Mom, I get it. Your body is made
> for outside. Mine is not.

"Mom, the craziest thing just happened! A butterfly landed on my balls!"

> Mom, I love you no matter what. Even if you were a zombie. I mean, we'd have to destroy you, of course, but we'd still love you. And we'd cut off your hand to keep as a souvenir to remember you always.

> Mom, I really like that my swim trunks have this mesh part in them so that minnows can't bite at my penis.

> "I love you, Mom!"
> "Aw! I love you too, sweetie!"
> "Um...okay...I was saying that to get you to go faster please."

> Mom, do you know why I love you so much? It's because you're so squishy.

> Mom, I wish I could just grow-up faster but without getting any taller.

> Mom, do girls have erections too?

> *calls from inside bathroom* Mom, just so you know, I think I'm hitting puberty.

> Mom, do I understand this correctly? So, a boy and a boy can't make a baby, but they CAN make enough money to adopt one, right?

Scientists

"Mom, when I drink through this straw, it's like there's a plastic tunnel sucking up water from the bottom of the cup into my mouth!"

"Mom, this smoothie tastes like real smoothies!"

> Mom, I got hit in the head by a tree!

> Mom, I think I'm allergic to my own farts.

"Mom, I found you this four-leaf clover, but a caterpillar ate one of the leaves off."

"Mom, this cheese smells like poop. I mean, I like it, but..."
"Well honey, when it comes to cheese, I always say 'the stinkier the better'."
"Cool. I guess I like poop then."

Mom, you know how they found that skeleton of the oldest human? Do you think they had any friends?

Mom, if you catch another mouse with that trap, can I please put it in a bag and take it to my teacher?

Mom, it's important to wait to brush your teeth after you eat chocolate, otherwise it's a very disturbing sight.

Mom, did you know that girls say more words than boys?

> Mom, if I were you, I wouldn't be drinking beer on my period. I mean...it's bad for you, and you're already feeling bad. Plus, it hurts your liver...which is close to your bladder... which is close to your vagina *mumbles* andallthatstuff. So it's just bad, and I wouldn't do it. Mkay, mom?

> "Look, Mom! I made a bladder. It's the first inside part I ever learned."

Existential Philosophers

> Mom, when I grow up, I don't know what I want to be. There are so many choices.

> Mom, sit down. I'm going to perform this rock song that I wrote. It's called 'I lost my dream'.

> Mom, is it always gonna be like this? Freedom? Like will freedom be the same when I grow up?

> Mom, when I'm at my dad's this week, can you just throw away all of my toys? I mean all of them, okay?! Except for that robot dinosaur, okay? And if you see any of those pull-back-and-go cars, keep those. And any of the remote control monster trucks, keep. And anything to do with building things. Or robots.

> Mom, I wish I had The Force.

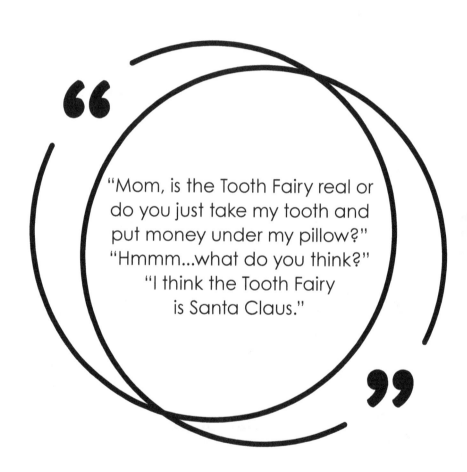

"Mom, is the Tooth Fairy real or do you just take my tooth and put money under my pillow?"
"Hmmm...what do you think?"
"I think the Tooth Fairy is Santa Claus."

> Mom, I had a nightmare, but I turned it into a video game instead. I only got attacked by one mutant spider.

> Mom, are hills really just Mother Nature's pimples?

Mom, why do rich people have so many bushes in front of their houses? They have like bush mazes and statues and stuff. Why do rich people have things like that?

Mom, I think there should be a movie called 'Government'.

"Mom, did you know that...on the other side of the world...a pizza just got baked?"

> Mom, in the future, like when I'm twelve, cars won't have wheels anymore. They'll just hover. And there won't be waitresses. They'll be robots instead, and they will make your coffee perfect. And they can throw pizza dough fifty feet in the air and catch it. And I hope you know that dragons aren't really real. They're basically just in video games.

> Lil Bro: "Mom, we HATE peace. Peace is just everybody sitting around. Peace is holding hands in a circle or whatever."
> Big Bro: "Nah, dude. You're thinking of meditation."

"Yeah Mom, that's why I don't drink tea. Cuz I don't trust companies."

"Mom, do you ever think about how our whole entire world might just be TV that another universe is watching?"

"Mom, smoke is actually made of spirits, and they're dancing into the mist."

"Mom, what is the point of life and existing and having cells? I mean, first we were fishes and now we have hands."

> Mom, what is our purpose for being here? Are we supposed to touch the stars or the bottom of the ocean? I just don't know.

> Mom, what do you think is going on when those dragonflies are connected to each other like that? I mean...I'm thinking it's some form of mind control.

> Mom, when I'm painting, I feel concentrated emotion. With this painting, I feel calm and excited, and I'm wondering why we are here and what is our purpose on Earth.

> Mom, does the government have a file on me?

> "Mom, I'm having bad dreams and can't sleep...Why is there war? And why do people want that much money?"

Forward Thinkers

> Mom, we gotta go downstairs and eat cereal--because it's Friday[3]!

> Mom, this present sounds like it has a cat inside of it. I think I need to open it now.

> Mom, can I please be on YouTube?

---

[3] We were listening to a lot of Rebecca Black. I mean, really, just the one song, but A LOT of it on repeat.

> Mom, tomorrow is my day to bring snacks for school. What do you think about asparagus, apples, and rosemary? Wouldn't that be great?

> Mom, I want to get glasses and braces (all silver) and be really smart. And I want to always carry around a pencil and a book to write down things when I learn them.

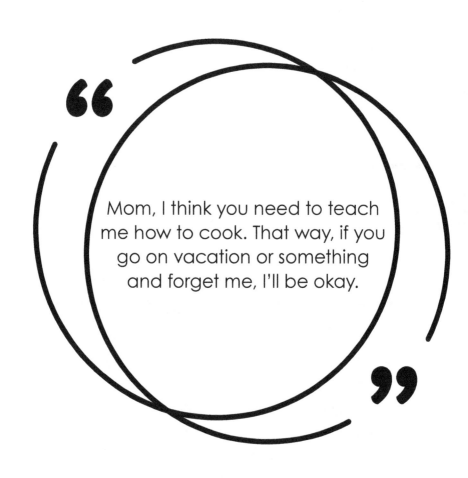

"Mom, I think you need to teach me how to cook. That way, if you go on vacation or something and forget me, I'll be okay."

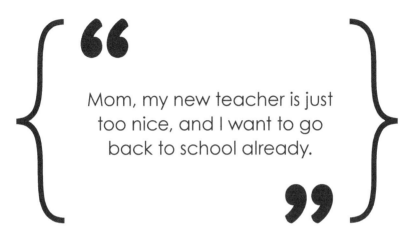

> Mom, my new teacher is just too nice, and I want to go back to school already.

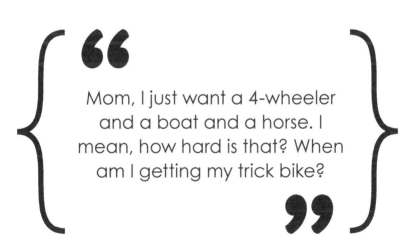

> Mom, I just want a 4-wheeler and a boat and a horse. I mean, how hard is that? When am I getting my trick bike?

> Mom, my favorite holiday is Christmas cuz you get stuff for free and don't gotta pay for things.

> Mom, I want to be on YouTube, get famous, and make lots of money.

"Mom, what do you think my talent is? Would you say it's 'being normal and stuff'?"

"Mom, there's a bunch of stuff in my take-home folder about things to do this summer, and I really want to show you this one thing. No, not that one. Nope, don't wanna go to wrestling camp. Not basketball. Where is it? Ah...here it is! Mom...I...want...to...dance!"

"Mom, can you please get me Dan TDM's phone number? I'd like to call him."

> Mom, I had the best day of my life today. You wanna know why? Cuz I discovered my singing voice.

> Mom, I'm tired of being judged for math and reading. I just wanna be a YouTuber.

Sweet, Sweet Angels

> "Mom, I smell the moon!"
> "Oh? What does it smell like?"
> "Breakfast bananas!"

> Mom, I'm gonna jump on you and hug you and kiss you! *slams into my face, covering it with snot, chocolate and slobber*

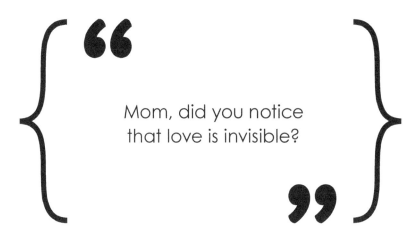

> Mom, did you notice that love is invisible?

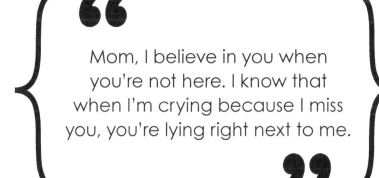

> Mom, I believe in you when you're not here. I know that when I'm crying because I miss you, you're lying right next to me.

> Mom, will you let me carry something? That way, things won't be so hard for you.

> Mom, I love you with all my heart, and if I had to, I'd go to the moon and save the space station and come right back to you.

> Mom, you look pretty like a gardener.

> Mom, I think Wednesdays should be called 'Wuddly Cuddly Wednesdays' and we just cuddle and love on each other and say nice things and wear pajamas.

> Mom, you should taste this. I think it tastes like love. *passes over Fun Dip*

> Mom, I spit on him because I LOVE YOU!

"Mom, I always want to make you happy, but sometimes I mess up."

"Please don't pee on anything outside the toilet!"
swirls stream back toward toilet
"Okay, Mom! Happy Mother's Day!"

Mom, you could be a snake charmer.

> Mom, I want to help[4] you as much as you help me.

> "Mom, I don't think I've ever treated you this way before with all these candles and massaging you with oils and stuff."
> "I don't think so either. You're making me feel really special!"
> "Well, you are special, Mom. YOU'RE KELLY STONE!"

---

[4] I was sick in bed, and he brought me tissues and tea.

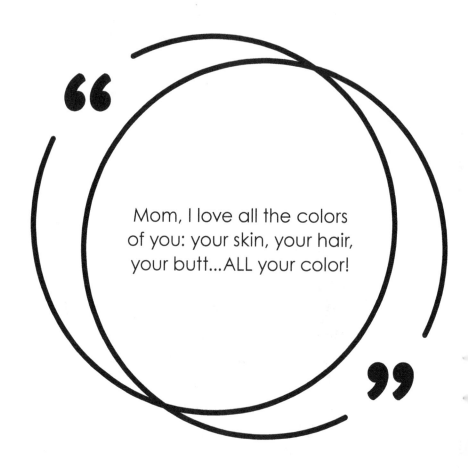

"Mom, I love all the colors of you: your skin, your hair, your butt...ALL your color!"

> Mom, my favorite part of you is your armpit. It's the warmest!

> Mom, I'm pretty sure you're a love ninja.

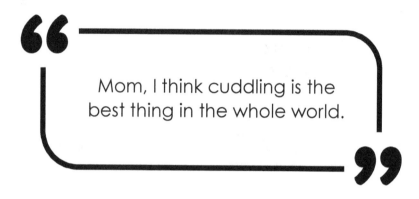

> Mom, I think cuddling is the best thing in the whole world.

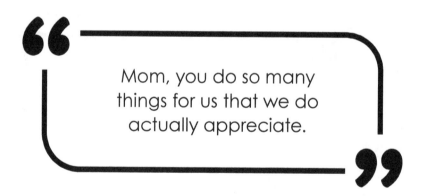

> Mom, you do so many things for us that we do actually appreciate.

Assholes

> Mommy, I love you, but why are you fat? Why are you so, so fat?

> Mom, one of the lunch ladies got a new hairstyle, and I told her it looked like a bunch of potatoes stacked up.

> Mom, I love you. Your belly is not as fat anymore.

> Mom, when *was* the last time you took a shower?

> Mom, why is your belly so big?

Mom, I kind of a little hate you, and I love you. It's like a compliment.

Mom, this dinner looks delicious--I mean--disgusting. Mmmm. I don't like the taste. I'm just eating it so fast cuz I'm hungry.

Mom, you should go back to Pre-K, and school, and college to learn how to use all your words.

Here, Mom, for your birthday, here's some candy we had at the house. Also, we filled your laptop with water.

Mom, if your stomach was more in and your boobs were more out, you'd look really pretty.

"Mom, you're skinny and a little bit fat, but you're tough."

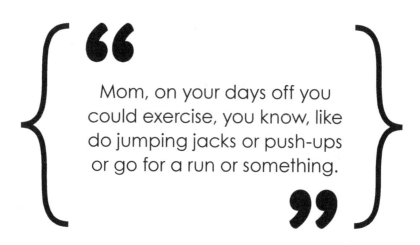

> Mom, on your days off you could exercise, you know, like do jumping jacks or push-ups or go for a run or something.

> Fine, Mom, I'll just be over here NOT EATING until you grate some cheese!

"Mom, if you didn't want mornings
to be stressful, you should
have only had one kid."

"Mom, your thigh is like a big turkey leg
that would take a really long time to eat."

> "Mom, I want you to know that I'm happy that you're not so annoying now."

"Mom, I was thinking. We don't need an alarm clock anymore. Instead, how about you start cooking us a nice good breakfast, and that way every day, I can wake up to the smell and the popping of bacon. Won't that be great?"

"Your thighs are too big and your belly pokes out. Mom, I'm not saying you're fat. I'm not saying that, but you do need to work out."

"Mom, I think for your New Year's resolution, you should be less talkie talkie about food."

> Mom, everyone in my class has a device they can download apps on. Either a laptop or a tablet or iPad. They're like $500. Pretty cheap. All I have is a GameBoy with some pretty boring games, and I can't download anything. I just want an iPad or a tablet. Or an XBox that works. I'm calling my dad!

> Mom, your toes[5] aren't looking that bad today.

---

[5] He gave me a toe ring for my birthday.

"Mom, I'm doing this so I won't be bored, and I won't complain."

{ " Mom, I'm tired of you telling us when to go to bed! I mean, WE ARE 8 AND 9! So, we're like almost teenagers, okay? " }

{ " Mom, I hate you. You treat me like I'm five, but I'm eight. And you know that's the same as twelve or eleven or thirteen. " }

> Mom, I wish you were still banned from Facebook.

> "Mom, are we going to a mall?"
> "No, we're actually going to a strip mall."
> "Oh...So that you could become a stripper?"

> "Hey Mom, I have an idea. How bout you give us a dollar every time you say 'clean'? Cuz we hate that word!"

Grossers

> Mom, I did put a lot of poop in my eye, but it never got pink.

> Mom, It's raining! Actually nope, just bird poop!

"Mom, I'm making something. It's food but also art."

"Mom, you know what? I would NOT like an alive doll."

"Mom, I decided to make some new rules for myself. No more eating in my bed. No more crumbs in my bed, and no spitting in my bed."

> Mom, we're not going to eat these bananas. They're house-flavored.

> Mom, I just used the potty, and I didn't even have to wipe. Come look at this tiny, tiny piece of poop that came out of me. It looks like the poo emoji.

> Mom, I just arm farted. Without my arm.

> Mom, there's something on the toilet seat that I made for you[6]. Come look!

> Mom, this tastes like the Queen of England's soap.

---

[6] It was my birthday.

In Mom's Shoes

> My boys just watched me perform comedy at a homeless shelter treatment facility. How hard did you mom today?

> While crossing the street with my children today, some crazy lady started screaming at me from her open truck window and told me to fellate my son and called me a whore. I really hated that my kids heard all this and that it stimulated questions about the inappropriate things she yelled. Then my youngest said "Mom, you just gotta shake off the haters," and I knew we were all gonna be just fine.

Today was kindergarten tours and registration. I asked my kid what I should wear so I could look like a mom that has a school-aged kid, and he said it didn't matter because they were gonna kick me out anyway.

No, baby. Just like in New Orleans... you don't lick the pole.

Guys, which one of you took apart my vagina[7]?

---

[7] It was a plastic vagina model.

> Today's moment of inspiration: My kid went to school wearing a soccer jersey with a clip-on tie.

> I hope this swimsuit top I'm wearing as a bra helps to look like I'm one of the "good" moms at this Kindergarten graduation.

> Tonight, I introduced my long-haired son to the concept of manbuns. After looking through @dailymanbun, he said, "Mom, I don't have a mustache or a beard to make it look cool."

> My little barfing baby woke up feeling grateful for his momma taking care of him last night and brought me pie and coffee in bed! He said, "I want you to feel like a queen."

> My 8-year old son just incorporated the most convincing impersonation of Gilda Radner into our conversation, and I couldn't possibly feel more momtastic.

Acknowledgements

I'm not sure how to go about thanking all the people that believed in me, this project, my kids, etc, but my gosh, your encouragement and validation has truly meant the world.

My friends—both real and interweb—made this happen. And my village, San Marcos, Texas. Of course, my offspring, the people I MADE, were the inspiration and content, so they should get some credit here. I also had editing help from Brandon Beck as well as all those people that I made thumb through the weird hardcopy I made and shoved into people's hands before they could say no! (SO MANY people). Thanks for helping me do this, Archway Publishing. Seriously, you've been amazing. And patient.

About the Author

Kelly Stone is a locally-famous[8] sex educator, comedian, and baby momma. She's performed in the Women in Comedy Festival, finished the Texas Water Safari, and given a TEDx Talk. She lives with her sons and their foster-fail pup, marveling daily at their in-

---
[8] 78666

sights, wisdom, and curiosities, while savoring the hearty laughs and warm hugs.

She's taught university for many years and travels the country to speak to a variety of health topics, yet she's still trying to figure out how to keep her kids from smearing Greek yogurt on the furniture.

To learn more about this author and to bring Kelly Stone to your community, organization or campus, please visit: kellystone.org

Kelly's still busy trying to stop her kids when they try to dart across a busy street. If you see them, lend a hand! There's safety in numbers, and it takes a village.

About the Boys

Mayne is fifteen months older than Denly because breastfeeding is not birth control. These guys are best friends who often need their space, and they enjoy video games, riding bikes, rivering, and (sigh) shooting guns. Someday, they each hope to have their own apartment and a decent job.

CPSIA information can be obtained
at www.ICGtesting.com
Printed in the USA
LVHW030017140521
687425LV00006B/218